2011

Change Management and Implementation Guide

Prepared By:

On Course Safety

oncoursesafety@gmail.com

12/6/2011

Change Management Plan

An Implementation Guide for the US Forest Service

Executive Letter

Fire and Aviation Managers,

As the US Forest Service Fire and Aviation Management continually strives to meet the demands of fighting wildland fires while providing the utmost safety processes, it is often faced with continuous changes to long standing systems and programs. As technology provides a springboard into new and better capabilities for the agency, it also provides challenges as these technologies or systems are introduced.

Change Management is a means of providing organization, structure, processes and guidance in implementing changes introduced either internally by the agency, or externally through changes in government regulations, etc. Managing these changes, as is required within a Safety Management Systems, provides a means to capture hazards that may be introduced into a program or system and manage people through the introduction and transition periods caused by change.

Traditionally change made to programs is performed at the management level and introduced to the field through training and implementation. The benefit of incorporating Change Management over traditional means of introducing change is that it provides critical safety controls through risk management processes, develops plans that meet management intent for the new system while ensuring the best methods for success are being implemented. It also provides a critical feedback link to management regarding safety assurance methods and whether or not the new technology or system is performing at the expected level. It provides for development of training and implementation as it prepares the workforce for transitions prior to the introduction of the change with early and often communication. And finally, it manages the process until the change has been fully introduced, is operational and the workforce has accepted it as the new way of doing things.

The Change Management and Implementation Guide is a tool for the agency to draw from during times of significant change. It is intended to be a guide that can be modified to meet each unique event while at the same time providing consistent structure to all changes introduced into the agency that may significantly impact a program, system or workforce.

The Change Management and Implementation Guide will bolster the current Safety Management System while contributing to improved management of changes and transition periods.

President
On Course Safety

Disclaimer

The information contained in this publication is subject to constant review in the light of changing government requirements, regulations and needs. No On Course Safety subscriber or other reader should act on the basis of any such information without referring to applicable laws and regulations and/or without taking appropriate professional advice. Although every effort has been made to ensure accuracy, On Course Safety and other resources shall not be held responsible for any loss or damage caused by errors, omissions, misprints or misinterpretation of the contents hereof. Furthermore, On Course Safety and resources to this publication expressly disclaim any and all liability to any person or entity, in respect of anything done or omitted, and the consequences of anything done or omitted, by any such person or entity in reliance on the contents of the publication.

The On Course Safety Change Management and Implementation Plan may only be reproduced, recast, reformatted or transmitted in any form by any means, electronic or mechanical, including photocopying, recording or any information storage and retrieval system, for expressed use of the On Course Safety subscriber for whom this manual was written.

The mention of specific resources in this publication does not imply that they are endorsed or recommended by On Course Safety in preference to others of a similar nature which are not mentioned.

TABLE OF CONTENTS

1.0   Introduction to Change Management

The purpose of this Change Management and Implementation Guide is to provide the US Forest Service's Fire and Aviation Management with pertinent information to help build a strategy when faced with an operational change. This includes change to the agency, a particular program or any other change that has potential to significantly impact personnel or operations whether originating from inside or outside the agency. As directed from the Chief's Safety Policy, *"The prevention of accidents can only occur if we commit to safe work practices, continually assess our changing environment, refuse to assume unacceptable risks, and continually address unsafe conditions"*.

Change often introduces hazards that are unknown or unforeseen due to the fact that something different has been introduced into a known and familiar method. In an attempt to proactively expose these hazards, a processed approach to introducing Change and managing people and systems through the transition period is a critical strategy for success.

This plan is dynamic and should be utilized to best meet the scope and scale of each change process. It should also be updated as better practices are identified. Knowledge gained through implementation as well as reviews during continuous improvement processes must contribute to additional versions of this plan. Revision control should be annotated on the Revision Control log within the US Forest Service Safety Management System Guide.

1.1 Safety Management System (SMS) Requirements for a Change Management Plan

Within the four components of SMS, the third component of Safety Assurance incorporates the process for managing change. The International Civil Aviation Organization (ICAO) and the Federal Aviation Administration (FAA) identify the management of Change as a key element of a Safety Management System (SMS). *FAA AC 120-92a, Element 3.2 "The organization will develop and maintain a process to identify changes within the organization or Its operational environment which may affect established processes and services and to describe the arrangements to assure safety performance before implementing changes[1]."* And finally the US Forest Service Aviation SMS Guide states *"The Washington Office (WO) Branch of Risk Management will identify and determine acceptable safety risk for changes within the organization which may affect established processes and services by new system design, changing system designs, new operations/procedures or modified operations/procedures[2]"*.

In order for SMS to be fully functional, it must include a plan for implementing Change within the organization.

1.2 What Changes Drive a Change Management Plan?

Not all changes to a system require a full Change Management Plan, so it is important to understand what triggers should be put in place that would activate a need for implementing Change Management.

---

[1] www.faa.fov/documentLibrary/media/Advisory_Circular/AC%2012-92a.pdf

[2] US Forest Service Aviation SMS Guide, Original page 25-26, dated 6/21/2011.

There are three specific conditions under which special attention for Change Management is warranted:

1. A problem is identified within the current operations often highlighted by an unexplained increase in safety related events or regulatory infractions.

2. Anytime a major operational change is foreseen, including;

   a. New system designs,
   b. Changes to existing system designs,
   c. New operations, procedures or programs,
   d. Modified operations, procedures or programs,
   e. Introduction of major equipment into an operation
   f. Changes to key personnel that could significantly impact an operation

3. Before or during periods of significant organizational change that includes rapid growth or downsizing and key personnel changes.

   a. This may be a result of either internal or external impacts to the organization.

1.3 Why the Management of Change is Important

The Change Management Plan aims to ensure that programs, systems, personnel and management are sufficiently prepared for change so they can operate to a satisfactory level of performance until the transition has been fully adopted and implemented. This plan applies principles and processes from SMS to manage specific hazards associated with change. As with SMS it entails both proactive processes such as risk assessment, mitigations and safety assurance processes, as well as reactive processes to identify deficiencies following adverse events associated with the change. Documentation of the change process must be recorded for safety assurance, continuous improvement and confidence that the process is still on track toward its goals and objectives.

1.4 Why Management of the Transition is Important

Transition and change is not the same thing. *"Change is situational: transition, on the other hand, is psychological."*[3] These are two different processes and each must be managed vigilantly in order for the desired modification to the system or program to be successful. Even with well designed and detailed plans put in place, the change can easily fail if the transition phase is ignored. It is imperative to manage people through the transitions that take place when change is introduced. Transitions travel through three distinct phases; The Ending, The Neutral Zone and the New Beginning.

Phase 1: *The Ending* – This is a period of letting go of the old way. Often there is an emotional tie, a sense of identity and a feeling of competence that is being removed from the current program or system.

---

[3] Bridges, W., Bridges, S., (2009), *Managing Transitions 3rd Edition, Making the Most of Change,* page 3, Da Campo Press, Philadelphia, PA.

Phase 2: *The Neutral Zone* – This is an in-between time, when the old way is gone but the new isn't fully operational. It is also a period when the workforce may feel least confident or comfortable in their positions. What used to be second nature and something they were good at is now creating feelings of inadequacy and doubt.

Phase 3: *The New Beginning* – This is when people develop the new identity, are competent again at their job and have made it through the change successfully with a new sense of purpose. This is the phase where the implemented change really begins to work.

If the transition isn't carefully planned and people aren't carefully managed through each phase, the change could take twice as long to implement or it may fail all together. Often managers rush through the transition periods or ignore them all together. Managers who have been a part of the change development and planning process are often at the New Beginning phase before the affected workforce even makes it into The Ending; hence they fail to recognize the emotional impact because they no longer feel the loss themselves.

1.5 Structure of the Change Management Plan

Since Change Management closely follows the Components, Elements and Process of SMS, the description of what those structures are is identified in SMS terms.

1. Change Management Policy and Objectives

    - Change Policy
    - Objectives of the Change Management Plan

2. Data Collection and Planning

    - Identification of the Problem
    - Management Commitment and Responsibilities
    - Change Management Accountabilities
    - Appointment of key personnel to the project
    - Gap Analysis
    - Incorporate a Communications Plan
    - Implement Documentation Process

3. Change Risk Management Processes

    - Define the Scope and Scale of the Operational Problem
    - Development of Hazard Identification Processes
    - Identification of Risk Assessment and Mitigations
    - Identification of a Benefit vs. Cost Process

4. Change Implementation Process

    - Phased or National Scope
    - Measurement of Success

5. Change Management Promotion Process

    - Change Management Communication processes

- Training in preparation for the Change implementation

6. Change Safety Assurance Processes

    - Monitoring of Change Activities and Methods
    - Data Gathering throughout the Change Implementation and Transition
    - Continuous Improvement to the Change Management Plan

7. Transition Management

    - Assessing Transition Readiness
    - Planning for the Transition
    - Developing a Transition Monitoring Team
    - The Leaders Role in Times of Transition

8. Change Management Documentation

    - Change policy and Objectives
    - Change processes and procedures
    - Accountabilities, responsibilities and authorities
    - Mechanism for ongoing involvement of management, implementation teams and program personnel
    - Change training programs, training requirements and attendance records
    - Change outputs of findings from implementation of Change and transition processes

9. Glossary specific to the Change being implemented

2.0 Change Management Processes

2.1 Change Management Process Step 1: Policy and Objectives

"Change of any sort succeeds or fails on the basis of whether the people affected do things differently".[4] Commitment by senior management (i.e. Director of Fire and Aviation, Assistant Director of Aviation and the National Risk Management Officer) to the change process is demonstrated to the organization by developing policies and standards for guiding change. The Change Management Policy is a very visible means of expressing commitment by leadership and encouraging participation throughout the organization. It is the primary channel of setting the tone for communication throughout the process and establishes support by providing sufficient resources to accomplish necessary objectives. The policy is the initial method of communication from leadership for change to the system or program. It identifies why Change Management is important, what methods and processes the organization intends to use to achieve the desired outcomes and how these methods and processes will be employed into operations.

The Change Management Policy should be approved at the senior manager level (i.e. Deputy Chief, State and Private Forestry) that has ultimate accountability and authority. It should be referred to often to ensure the process is meeting the course of action laid out by leadership. The policy is a call to action for the implementation of change and lends leadership support and direction to the entire process.

---

[4] Bridges, W., Bridges, S., (2009), *Managing Transitions 3rd Edition, Making the Most of Change,* page 6, Da Campo Press, Philadelphia, PA.

Change Management Policy

1. Defines senior management's (i.e. Director, Fire and Aviation Management) commitment to the Change Management process.

2. Defines roles, responsibilities and accountabilities of directors, managers and employees.

   a. Who (i.e. Deputy Chief, State and Private Forestry) can direct, control, or change the procedures and make key decisions regarding safety risk acceptance.

   b. The policy defines lines of authority and accountability, communication, procedures, and responsibility by the organization, the program or system, and employees.

3. Defines the purpose of the change within the program or system.

   a. How change may affect established processes and services.

   b. Awareness of the potential for hazards to be introduced into an operation whenever change occurs.

   c. Awareness that change could affect the appropriateness and effectiveness of existing safety risk mitigation strategies.

4. Defines the objectives that meet the purpose of the change and allow for modifications to the objectives to ensure the purpose is accomplished.

5. Identifies the scope, methods and processes for the change.

6. Defines the outputs expected from managers and the team.

7. Should align with the Safety Management System Policy and other operational policies.

8. Secures commitment and involvement from all necessary staff.

9. Secures commitment by the organization to provide the necessary resources for successful Change Management.

10. Ensures the performance is measurable against the Change Management Plan.

11. Defines oversight and management of the transition processes.

2.2 Objectives for the Change Management Plan

The objectives set the operational Change Management standards. They must be specific, measurable realistic and agreed with by those who have to deliver them. Ensure the objectives are approved by the accountable senior manager (i.e. Director, Fire and Aviation Management).

1. Set short and long term objectives that will continue to direct the Change Management process through the transition period.

2. Set indicators and targets the will keep the process on track to achieve the objectives.

---

3. Communicate the objectives to foster a common understanding of what the Change Management Process is set to achieve.

3.0 Change Management Process Step 2: Data Collection and Planning

3.1 Identify the Problem

Problems are what normally lead to a change. When a problem is recognized at a level where it requires consideration for change implementation, begin a preliminary information gathering and documentation process. It is important to recognize which program or systems to which the Change Management Process pertains as well as other programs or systems that may be impacted. The problem should be sufficiently identified and preliminary actions recorded.

1. What is the problem, event or catalyst that is creating a decision leading toward this change?

2. What program or system does the problem and eventual change apply to?

3. Collect information about the problem from those closest to it.

4. Engage people in the problem-solving process.

   - Gain peoples investment in the process which will in turn gain their interest in the outcome.

   - Work to acquire the influence of the most effective and respected people within that system or program.

   - Try to understand what interests are currently in place that people might try to protect when facing transitions caused by this change.

5. Communicate the problem throughout the system, program or organization to begin the process of allowing people to prepare for the transition. Don't wait until the change is just about to be implemented.

3.2 What are the Required Resources?

The problem has been identified. Now what resources will be required to begin the change process?

4. Who is the National Director, Fire and Aviation Manager or Line Officer who has ultimate responsibility and accountability for the program or system?

5. Who are those within the system or program who have the most knowledge?

6. Who has the safety responsibilities, accountabilities and authority?

7. How much time will be required for;

   - Information gathering
   - Planning
   - Implementing
   - Transitioning

8. What are the contingency plans in case a critical event takes place due to the problem before the problem can be fully addressed.

3.3 The Change Management Action Team

Once the resources have been identified, select members for the Change Management Action Team. These members must have an appropriate experience base, represent each line of the system or operation and be able to see the process to completion from planning, to implementation and through the transition phases. It is possible to have a separate Transition Management Team, however, ensure there are members of the Change Management Action Team who will provide a consistent link throughout the process. A Terms of Reference document for the Change Management Action Team will help define the group's purpose, who they are directly responsible to, who the members should be. It should define the group's tasks, budget parameters and team outputs. Here are some terms to consider:

1. Identification of the Change Management Action Team

   - Size of the team will depend on the scope and scale of the Change Project.
   - Ensure the experience base of the individuals is appropriate for the project.
   - Provide Change Management and Transition Management training or orientation for the group to ensure understanding of the team's tasks and challenges in guiding the Change process.

2. Duties of the Change Management Team

   - Assigning Roles and Responsibilities (leadership, communication plan, documentation, etc.)
   - Facilitating a Gap Analysis (what processes are already in place to handle the new system and what areas need to be developed)
   - Development of the Change Management Plan
   - Detailed planning for further Change Management processes
   - Development of the Change Implementation Plan
   - Facilitate the progress of the Implementation Plan
   - Develop the Transition Management Plan
   - Implement the Change Safety Assurance processes
   - Ensure the transition throughout the three phases is closely monitored and managed.

3.4 Change Management Documentation Processes

The documentation describes all the elements of the Change Management Plan and provides record of Change Management activities and adjustments to the plan during the implementation process. Its purpose is a centralized location for all those who need to consult the information, to provide a means of historical data in order to capture the starting point and a continuous improvement resource for updates and upgrades to the plan. This should include at a minimum:

1. Problem Identification documents

2. Change Management Policies and Objectives

3. Change Management Processes and Procedures

4. Change Management Action Team Terms of Reference

5. Change Management Risk Assessment and Mitigations

   - Hazard Identification Processes
   - Risk Assessment Processes
   - Mitigation Measures Applied
   - Determination of Cost and Benefit of mitigations

6. Change Quality Assurance and Safety Assurance Processes

   - Data Collection and Review of Processes
   - Performance Evaluation of Change Processes
   - Identification of Emerging Hazards from Change Implementation
   - Improvement Measures for Effectiveness of the Change Management Plan

7. Change Management Communication Plan and Outputs

8. Change Management Training Programs and Outputs

9. Change Management Implementation Plan and Outputs

10. Transition Management Plan and Outputs

11. Change Management Outputs and results of the Change Management Process

3.5 Conduct a Gap Analysis

A gap analysis is a tool to help determine what policies, procedures, guides, manuals, training, and other arrangements which are already in place and might readily receive the change and where there are holes or "gaps" that may require further development. The gap analysis may also help determine where there are vulnerabilities that arise as consequences of the introduction and interaction between people and the specific features of the change.

The organization will need to design the Gap Analysis Checklist to specifically meet the unique needs of the program or system being affected. There are several sources to draw from when developing the checklist.

1. Utilize the Fire and Aviation Safety Management System Office for Quality Assurance Audit Checklist and other resources. These may provide detailed information for items that may be appropriate to or modified for the Gap Analysis Checklist.

2. Review the FAA SMS Gap Analysis checklist. This source provides both preliminary and detailed Gap Analysis information for reference on format and safety content[5].

3. ICAO Gap Analysis Safety Management Manual.

Once the Gap Analysis is complete, ensure it is well detailed and incorporated into the documentation process. The items that are identified as missing or deficient will then form the

---

[5] http://www.faa.gov/about/initiatives/sms/specifics_by_aviation_industry_type/air_operators/

basis for the Change Management Plan which will ensure the implementation will address these items.

4.0   Change Management Process Step 3: Risk Management and Criticality of Change

4.1   Introduction to Change Risk Management

This process should start by answering the question of "how important is the equipment or activity to safe system operations"? Change Risk Management processes, which are very similar to SMS risk management processes, are intended to manage the specific hazards that may be introduced by the change that is taking place within the program. The SMS risk management processes manage all risks within a program. The Change Risk Management process is specifically designed to manage the risks related to and introduced by the changes implemented into and impacting a program or system. *"Criticality relates to the potential consequences of equipment being improperly operated or an activity being incorrectly executed"*[6]. Ensure the criticality of a system or activity is addressed alongside hazard and risk management.

4.2   Identification of Hazards Introduced by Change

The risk management process for the introduction of a change within a program or system needs to identify what hazards are introduce or may be hidden within the system. The hazard identification process must work to reveal these hazards and then assess the level of risk these hazards present. Once this has taken place the development of mitigations and controls for these hazards needs to be determined. Once the controls have been identified and rated for residual risk, the final step is to determine the cost of each mitigation measure and the level of benefit it provides to the systems.

There are three processes that help reveal hazards:

4. **Predictive**

    The predictive process shall identify change hazards by known affects of a particular introduction to a program. An example of this would be the national implementation of internal cargo in the rappel program. It is a known and highly utilized existing process that has been introduced to units that were accustomed to external cargo.

5. **Proactive**

    The proactive process identifies hazards within the current program or system that may exceed current controls if a change is introduced. These are identified through employee reporting systems, surveys, program data that may be available through annual reports, manufacturer information and other available sources.

---

[6] ICAO Safety Management Manual www.icao.int/anb/safetymanagement/DOC_9859_FULL_EN.pdf

6. **Reactive**

Since it is very difficult to identify all hazards when introducing something new, the reactive process is key to gathering hazard information that can only be identified when it has been put into operation for a period of time. The important aspect of this process is to ensure that well planned monitoring processes are put into place:

- After Action Reviews are documented and analyzed for common situations that are becoming concerns.

- Verification of the risk assessment and its mitigation measures. What may have been missed during the process?

- A monitoring process that will ensure risks are being managed as anticipated.

- If the change involves a product or new tool, ensure communication and feedback to the manufacturer is part of the process. Tools that have been introduced to the field without a monitoring process often can created work-arounds and potentially more serious hazards (i.e. new gas containers for fueling chain saws in the field). If the product is not working as anticipated, it needs to be addressed.

4.3 Assessing Risk

The risk assessment process is the means of placing a rating of probability and severity to the identified change-induced or related hazards. These hazards are linked to a particular system within the program such as Personnel or Equipment and then each system's hazards are assessed. [7]

4.4 Hazard Mitigation

Risk mitigation is the processes of assigning controls to the hazards that have been identified. It is important to designate meaningful controls that will affect either the probability of the hazard occurring or the severity if the hazard occurs or both. Each mitigation measure is then rated again for its affect on the probability and severity of the hazard.

4.5 Benefit and Cost of Control Measures

The final rating should consider what affects the mitigations have on the outcome of the hazard. Once each mitigation measure is rated for its overall risk score, the mitigation is to be assessed for the benefit it provides to control the risk associated with the hazard. The final step is to then determine the cost and rate the particular mitigation measure from a Cost/Benefit rating chart[8]. If the cost of the mitigation is high and the benefit is low, the overall rating would be poor for

---

[7] Good resources exist within the Forest Service Fire and Aviation Management's Aviation Safety Management System Guide and the strategic program risk assessments located on the Fire and Aviation Safety site on the US Forest Service website to provide examples of two different styles of risk matrixes.

[8] Again, reference the resources that exist within the Forest Service Fire and Aviation Management's Aviation Safety Management System Guide and the strategic program risk assessments located on the Fire and Aviation Safety site on the US Forest Service website to provide examples of Cost/Benefit rating scales.

the implementation of that mitigation. It may still be a required implementation measure, but maybe lower on a priority list.

5.0   Change Management Process Step 4: Change Management Promotion

This component of Change Management as mirrored through Safety Management Systems, addresses training processes associated with changes and communication plans. This promotion process supports the core operational activities of the Change Management Plan.

5.1 Change Management Communication Plan

The Change Management process must be clearly communicated in order to ensure continuous support and commitment by leadership, the Change Management Action Team and the workforce within the program or system affected. Communicate the reason for the change by actually "selling the problem". Do it early and often before you try and share the change itself. the problem, and the change process is clearly understood by those in the planning process, leadership and the workforce that the Change will eventually impact, it must be properly communicated.

The Change Management training is an important part of the communications plan. However, training usually occurs at particular intervals (i.e. annually) and may not be convenient for necessary information events. The communication plan should:

1. Explain the Change Management policies, procedures and responsibilities to those involved

2. Describes the channels of communication used to gather and disseminate Change Management information.

3. Identify triggers that should activate an information flow for both anticipated and unanticipated events.

The communication plan continually provides ongoing information regarding activities and safety performance and encourages continued commitment by the program, system or community the change is affecting. Consider a variety of means when developing the plan; electronic media such as email, twitter, websites, social media accounts (i.e. Google Plus and Facebook) as well as traditional communication through newsletters, bulletins, seminars and training events. Continually be looking for new and useful methods of communication that may benefit the information sharing process.

The information disseminated must be timely, clearly understood and credible. It should be specific to the intended group so they are not overloaded with irrelevant information that may create a lack of interest and eventually a lack of participation. The goal is to keep people engaged, not overburden them.

Information relies on feedback in order for it to be communication. Feedback from the program, system or community is necessary to achieve the objectives of the plan as well as having the ability to understand the impacts during the phases of the transition periods. Feedback requires confidence in the system and an assurance that information will be used appropriately. Policies should be specific regarding data confidentiality and the ethical use of information provided by the program, system or field.

Feedback from the field provides valuable information to the Change Management Plan, not only in recognizing the progress of the plan, but in adjusting tactics as necessary to continue toward success. It also is a tool that provides learning events for future Change Management Plans and the continuous improvement process. In order to keep the feedback system healthy, responses to field reports needs to be identified in the communication plan. If people don't receive timely responses with some indication of follow-up activity, they may stop participating rendering the communication process ineffective.

5.2 Training associated with the Implemented Change

Training regarding the proposed change should involve all personnel associated with that particular program or system to ensure they are competent to undertake the responsibilities. Though they may be competent coming out of the training, they may not feel confident which should be of concern to management and is addressed in the Transition section of this document. Key aspects of training for change are the special features and aspects that require unique knowledge and understanding relevant to their roles within the program. Here are considerations for training:

1. Who needs to be trained?

2. How will the training plan or curriculum be developed?

3. Are there different consideration for crews, teams and individuals?

4. What are special training considerations for the Change Management Action Team and the Transition Management Team?

5. What training should be considered for senior management regarding the change and transition plans and processes?

6. Determine frequency of training for a phased approach to change implementation.

7. Determine considerations and logistics for national implementation approach.

8. Determine re-currency requirements if necessary.

9. Develop knowledge check strategies to ensure understanding.

10. Develop training documentation and record keeping processes.

6.0 Change Management Process Step 5: Implementing Change

Each Change that it implemented into a system must be addressed individually with each unique process that presents itself. Not every Change Plan will work for every situation; some change processes can be implemented all at once, while others will require implementation in stages. The stage or phased approach is often considered for the larger changes where it can tested, evaluated, adjusted and then expanded to other areas. Either way, ensure the implementation of the change does not outpace the resources or plan. This would likely ensure a complete loss of boundaries and controls during the transition period and a high potential of failure.

6.1 Phased Change Implementation at the Regional or Forest Level:

This should be a well designed method of introducing the change into a system or program. The more complex an introduction of a change to a system on a large scale, the more consideration should be given to setting controls and sideboards on the implementation. Should the implementation be restricted early on to a Forest Level, a Regional Level or can it be effectively implemented nationally while still maintaining control of the implementation and the transition. There are benefits and drawbacks to each method.

Benefits of Phased Approach:

1. Tightly controlled processes. Can be used as a "test bed" to learn and improve the implementation prior to going national with the change.

2. Keeps the change to a manageable size so that if the change begins to negatively affect the workforce or safety of the program it can be quickly addressed and managed.

3. Helps improve the Change Management Plan and its implementation once all "kinks" have been worked out of the system in the smaller scope of a Forest or Region.

4. A more improved plan can be implemented on a national level and management is more aware of the challenges it will face at a national level. Fewer surprises and more capability to implement and manage the transitions.

5. If there are any failures to the change process, the financial impact would be less significant at a Forest or Regional Level.

Drawbacks of Phased Approach:

1. Implementation and transition of the overall change will take longer to fully accomplish nationally.

2. Misinformation and inaccurate information could leak through the "grapevine", impacting the Transition Readiness of other Forests or Regions when the change does go national.

3. May not provide enough data to fully understand how it will impact an entire program or system nationally.

6.2 National Implementation Considerations

Implementing a full scale change throughout an organization or on a national level can be a logistically difficult undertaking. The plan, resources, key personnel and Change Management Action Team need to ensure all aspects are well prepared for such a large undertaking. That being said, the entire program or system will experience the change together.

Benefits of National Implementation:

1. The implementation will be conducted all at once potentially decreasing the transition time to becoming fully operational.

2. A quality Communication Plan would greatly enhance information sharing between Forest or Regions as the changes and transitions begin to reveal better or more efficient processes.

3. There should be a large pool of information to analyze data gathered on a larger scaled implementation.

Drawbacks of National Implementation:

1. Would likely be more expensive to implement on a large scale at one time.

2. May not have sufficient human and other resource required to appropriately manage the change.

3. Limited ability of oversight as the change could be implemented extensively on units, forests, bases, systems, etc. significantly impacting controls.

4. Communication and information may be impacted due to the extensive workforce that must be provided accurate information. Keeping up with and managing the "grapevine" could prove difficult.

6.3 Measurement of Success

It is important to understand if the change introduced has made the desired impact to the program. If there is no means to become aware of any deficiencies of the new system or negative impacts it may have on the work of personnel within the program, there is no way to capture and provide for improvement. There are specific means to acquire such information:

1. Ensure the workforce is aware of a reporting and feedback system and encourage them to disclose any glitches in the system or work-arounds that might be developing.

2. Gather data sources that were defined within the Change Management Plan and look for trends or concerns that may be arising due to the introduction of change.

3. Encourage site visits to locations impacted by the change to determine if current training programs are providing sufficient information and capabilities to the workforce.

4. Evaluate communication capabilities and whether or not the field or workforce was provided accurate and timely information.

5. Determine if the change and transition periods accomplished the objectives and met the leaders intent for change implementation.

6. Update the Change Management Plan and implementation processes to better ensure success for future changes to agency programs and systems.

7. Gain insight from personnel attitudes and comfort levels as the transition periods are moving forward. This can be done through surveys or interviews, but it is important to gather information on the "psychological and emotional health" of the workforce experiencing the change.

7.0 Change Management Process Step 6: Change Safety Assurance

The Change Safety Assurance process is the performance of monitoring activities and data analysis that provide feedback regarding controls and mitigations. It is the primary source for evaluating effectiveness of controls as they are put into action in the field. This is an additional layer of defense that is a validation of risk control expectations and a confirmation of objectives for the Change Management Plan.

7.1 Assigning Responsibility for Change Safety Assurance Processes

Some of the change safety assurance processes can be undertaken by the Change Management Action Team, while others may be undertaken by individuals. The Change Management Action Team or Transition Management Team can identify what data needs to be collect and by whom. Another source is to identify individuals within the program who are subject matter expert in that particular field. This source of data collection would be beneficial in:

1. Observation of operations as they take place in the field.

2. Conducting and managing After Action Reviews.

3. Verifying the risk assessment in the field.

4. Being the primary point of communication feedback from the field to back to the Action Team and Management.

5. Provide the source for documentation of emerging hazards and trends.

7.2 Collect and Review Change Data

The data collected should be identified within the Change Management Plan. There are several means of gathering pertinent change implementation data for monitoring the safety performance of the introduced change.

1. Hazard reporting systems

2. Accident and Incident reports

3. Review the Change Readiness Audit results conducted prior to the implementation of the change.

4. Conduct After Action Reviews and document and analyze findings.

7.3 Evaluate the Performance of the Change Implementation

A primary finding for Change Safety Assurance, is whether or not the change implementation is meeting the objectives defined in the policy. If targets are not being met that are intended to keep the change on track, feedback through the system should trigger activation in the Change Management Plan to modify activities in order to meet the objectives.

1. Continually monitor performance of the Change Management Plan and its implementation processes to validate effectiveness.

2. Eliminate or modify risk controls that have unintended consequences or have run their course and are no longer needed.

3. Ensure feedback is built into the system to provide for positive communication to management and the workforce.

4. Verify the risk assessment process through observations and other methods of the change as it is being used in the field or workforce.

7.4 Identify Emerging Hazards from the Change Implementation

An additional function is the evaluation of change performance indicators and emerging hazard that begin to sift through as the change to operations or field applications gain momentum. These findings are then fed back into the Change Risk Assessment as a reactive process and mitigated or controlled as per the Change Management Plan.

It is also a means of identifying any changes that may be taking place within the operating environment that were not anticipated in the Change or Implementation Plan. Planning for the change is one thing, but external and unanticipated changes to the environment that may directly or indirectly affect the targets and objectives of the change is quite another. This would again feed back into the Change Risk Assessment as a reactive process to be controlled through mitigation measures.

1. Identify the most efficient and effective processes and design them back into the Change Management Plan for continuous improvement.

2. Identify and document areas of most significant concern that can be addressed up front during any subsequent changes implemented into the organization, program or system.

Finally, the Change Safety Assurance process provides input to the ways of improving the implementation of change within systems and programs. These evaluation and data gathering methods provide for the continuous improvement aspect to the Change Management Plan.

8.0 Managing the Transition: A Simultaneous Process

8.1 What is the Transition Period and Why Does It Matter?

The Transition Period is the time and process by which people get through change. Though each change is different and is full of unknowns, the transition process is well mapped and understood. Each change comes with transition, and each transition proceeds through three different phases. Knowing this and preparing to manage the transition process is a well marked path in charting a way through change.

Now that the decision has been made to implement a change, the matter of preparing and managing the workforce is an equally important process. These are the people that must perform within the Change Plan, and if they aren't well informed, managed and recognized as the key to successful change, the entire plan may fall well short of its goals and objectives. The three phases of Transition that people must be helped through are The Ending, The Neutral Zone and The Beginning.

8.2 Phase I: The Ending

Whenever there is a change implemented into an organization, employees and managers alike have to let go of something. Endings create a loss or require letting go of something and that is where management will find themselves dealing with resistance. It isn't the change necessarily that people are resisting as much as the loss they are experiencing. This isn't the phase to talk about how good and healthy the change is going to be, but rather deal directly with the losses and endings. *The single biggest reason organizational changes fail is that no one has thought about endings or planned to manage their impact on people[9]*. These are the items to consider when planning for this first phase of Transition:

1. Identify who is losing what.

   - Provide the difficult information up front and provide it in as much detail as possible.
   - Is there something that is over for everyone?

2. Don't be surprised by overreaction.

   - People are losing a piece of their world, not a piece of yours. It will take time for them to process.

3. Acknowledge the losses openly and express concern.

   - Pretending the loss doesn't exist stirs up more trouble than talking about it.

4. Expect and accept signs of grieving.

   - These emotional states can be mistaken for bad morale when in fact people are really feeling a loss.

5. Is there a way to compensate for the loss?

   - If the change is taking a feeling of competence and replacing it with uncertainty, try to find a way to give them back a sense of control.

6. Give people information, early and often.

   - The typical lines of communication throughout a program may not provide the most accurate or timely information.
   - Ensure the message gets out and gets out to the targeted people; early and often.
   - If you don't know the information on particular events, give them a time you will know and stick to it. If the information still isn't available at the particular date, let them know it still isn't available. Don't let the date just go by, keep the commitment.

7. Define what is over and what isn't.

   - Leaders must not shy away from specifying what is over and what isn't.
   - Put into words what goes and what stays in each aspect of the change.

8. Mark the endings.

   - There is a point of no turning back. Mark this "line in the sand" in some way that can be meaningful and memorable.

9. Treat the past with respect

   - If the past is not treated with respect, there is a risk of creating more resistance. Honor the past for what it has accomplished.

---

[9] Bridges, W., Bridges, S., (2009), *Managing Transitions 3rd Edition, Making the Most of Change*, page 37, Da Campo Press, Philadelphia, PA.

10. Let people take a piece of the old way with them.

   - The point is to disengage people from the past not to rip it from them. Find a way to let them take a piece of their past with them.

11. Show how endings ensure continuity of progress.

   - The way things are done today was a product of changes of the past. Tomorrow's changes lead the way to the future.

8.3 Phase II: The Neutral Zone

The Neutral Zone is the period after the change implementation has begun; the old ways are gone but the new way isn't comfortable yet or working satisfactorily. This is where management could get impatient with the amount of time it seems to be taking for the change to be fully operational and effective. This is a very difficult time both for the organization and for the workforce.

Here are some concerns to watch for in the Neutral Zone:

1. People's effectiveness falls.

2. People tend to miss more work or begin looking elsewhere for work.

3. Old problems that may have been improving can reemerge.

4. Priorities become confusing and turn-over can rise.

5. Teamwork can be undermined and people can become polarized.

6. People become disorganized and tired and may become slow to recognize or respond to safety concerns and threats.

Tips to manage this precarious time:

1. Normalize this time in this "no-man's-land".

   - Encourage reorientation and redefinition of outlooks, attitudes and values within the organization. Don't just wait for this period to pass like there is nothing to be done about it.

2. Redefine the Neutral Zone as a time of opportunity.

   - Though things aren't yet as they should be, this is a time to let people be creative in preparing for their new future. A time when improvements can be made that have long been requested. Small victories in this time will help people pass through it more successfully.

3. Provide structure and strength during the Neutral Zone.

   - Protect people from further change or delay new changes until they are more prepared to handle it.
   - Consider implementing task forces or project teams to help manage, communicate or encourage throughout the Neutral Zone.

- Set short-range goals and check points along the way.
- Ensure leadership has provided the information to understand and succeed in the Neutral Zone.
- Be wary of showing preference of one group over another. Special treatment causes trouble, but people will put up with a lot if everyone is in the same boat together.

4. Use a Transition Monitoring Team (TMT)

- The is a vital tool for several reasons;
  - o TMT can provide unfiltered communication to leadership from the field.
  - o TMT is made from a cross-section of the program or organization.
  - o It is an effective focus group that reviews communication effectiveness.
  - o Used to counter misinformation and rumors.
  - o Is familiar with the phases of transitions and can catch concerns before they get out of hand.

The Neutral Zone is a time where people must be protected, encouraged, given structure and opportunities. If they are afforded these, people will work the rest out for themselves.

8.4 Phase III: The New Beginning

This phase is marked by new energy and confidence. People have moved passed the loss and grieving of letting go, sorted out their place and future within the change process and are now at a point where they once again feel comfortable in their work.

Actions that will take people from the Neutral Zone into The Beginning is that they have been part of an effective communication process throughout all phases. Being fed information on the purpose of change early and often, provided a mental picture of what their world should look like when it is all said and done, informed on the plan to get the change implemented and finally what part or role they play in it brings people along more effectively.

Purpose:

The purpose for the change usually grows from a problem that was identified. This problem and reason for consideration and implementation of the change should be communicated effectively. If people don't understand the purpose, roadblocks and hurdles may hinder the Change Plan and progress.

Picture:

Provide a picture in the head of the workforce so they can understand what their world will look like once the change is implemented. The picture is the reality of where people are in their work, once they lose the old picture it is important they can visualize what their new world will look like.

The Plan:

The Transition plan differs from the Change Plan in that it addresses change from the personal level rather than the organizational level. It provides structure and outlines things like key events, information, training and where people can find support throughout the process.

The Transition plan starts with where people currently are and works forward to where the organization wants them to be.

Part to Play:

People need to understand their role in the change process and what their relationship is in contributing to the process. What role do they play will help them have an investment in the outcome of the change implementation. They also need to understand how they can deal effectively with the transition management process.

1. When people understand the problem, they become invested in the solution.

2. Providing people with the information without hiding things from them will help align people and management on one side and the problem on the other.

3. People are an enormous wealth of knowledge and skill. By including them in the process, their knowledge becomes available to decision-makers.

4. Providing people with a role to play brings their energy to the table. Instead of sitting back waiting to be told what to do next or what is next in the plan, they already have the information and are moving through the transition phases with the purpose they have been provided by management.

8.5 The Leaders Role in Times of Transition

In Dr. William Bridges book *Managing Transitions 3rd Edition,* his emphasis of not just managing the transition period, but leading people through it is the most essential aspect of ensuring successful change can take place. *"When yesterdays changes leave such a legacy of resentment, today's changes are undermined even before they are launched.*[10] If the organization is known for pushing change without considering the impact it has on the workforce, it will be a very real and uphill battle to move the next change through successfully. Dr. Bridges points out that there are five measurable costs to the workforce and even at different levels of management if managing the transition is not done effectively. These costs are generally represented through attitudes; guilt, resentment, anxiety, self-absorption and stress. It is up to leadership to determine how they can encourage a vibrant and effective workforce, instead of a disgruntled group that will eventually either get the change or leave. How leadership manages the transition will determine the outcome.

8.6 Planning the Transition

Making a fully effective plan for the transition may not be as easy as the plan for the change. The fact that it entails the dynamic nature of people, many of which may not be such willing participants, is going to present some challenges and modifications along the way. However, ignoring it is a recipe for failure. The following items will assist in building an initial transition plan.

---

[10] Bridges, W., Bridges, S., (2009), *Managing Transitions 3rd Edition, Making the Most of Change,* page 140, Da Campo Press, Philadelphia, PA.

1. **Share the Problem** – This is a key item that should already be incorporated into the Communications Plan. Selling the problem is fundamental to preparing the workforce for the transition. Don't share the change until the problem has been thoroughly "sold" to those it will affect.

2. Collect information about the problem. What is it about the current situation that people may be opposed to losing?

3. Conduct the audit or an evaluation of the program's readiness for the transition process.

4. Educate leadership on the differences between change and transition.

5. Ensure the Change Management Action Team is knowledgeable and prepared to understand who is going to have to let go of something and how they can manage and encourage people through it.

6. Recognize and plan for each of the three phases of the transition. To ignore any one of them in order to rush the change through will only disrupt, delay or defeat the change process.

7. Re-evaluate how the change plan and transition process are going. Probably the best time to do this is during the second phase of the transition, the Neutral Zone. This is a point where the Action Team can evaluate how well the change and transition is going. It is a point where strategies and resources are reviewed and objectives can be adjusted to better meet the purpose of the change.

8. If the Change Management Action Team does not have the capability or resources to effectively manage the entire process all the way through the transitions, assign a Transition Monitoring Team. This will enable the Action Team to gain progress reports from the field as the changes and transitions take place without over- burdened them and thus making them less effective.

9. Plan how the team is going to explain, encourage and even reward the new behavior and attitudes that the changes are going to require of people.

10. Throughout the entire process, keep track of what helps and what hinders the organization and its people as they go through the transition. This will provide valuable continuous improvement information not only for the current changes being implemented, but for future changes to the organization and other programs.

8.7 Assessing Transition Readiness

Within the Change Management Plan, the problem that was the catalyst for the change being implemented was identified. The importance of identifying and recognizing the problem is so the Change Management Plan can be built on a strong foundational purpose for the implementation of the change. Change involves developing a means of placing something new into a current system or program to address a given problem. The transition is the result of incorporating that change into the system which then impacts the people within a particular program.

The assessment of transition readiness can be a very informal process with the intent to get a sense of how ready those within a program are to handle change. It can be done through conversations with individuals, surveys, or other data gathering devices. If the climate of the workforce is found to be incapable of handling the change, trying to force them through the transition of a change that was supposed to strengthen the program may actually end up weakening it.

Change Management and Implementation Guide

Here is a list of questions that will help the organization understand its transition readiness. The important aspect of this assessment process is to get feedback from as wide a set of sources as possible.

Evaluating the organizations readiness. [11]

1. Is there a sense among the workforce that a change is necessary to address a known problem?
2. Do most people accept that whatever change is taking place represents a valid and effective response to the underlying problem?
3. Does the proposed change polarize the workforce in any way that will make the transition more disruptive?
4. Is the level of trust in the organizations leadership adequate? If it is low, it will be very difficult to bring people along.
5. Will the organization provide people with adequate training for the new situation and roles?
6. Does the organization have a healthy "Just Culture" that allows for mistakes within a new situation?
7. Is there a means to capture mistakes and their affects and mitigate them?
8. Does the change fit into a widely understood strategy with a fairly clear vision of the future?
9. Do people understand why they will have to be letting go of existing systems? Is it talked about publically?
10. Is the cultural memory of the organization open to change or has it been scared by past failures?
11. Has the change been explained to those who are going to be affected by it in as much detail as is currently possible?
12. Are there people within the organization who have experience in change and transition management?
13. Do the leaders of the change understand that the *transitions* will take considerably longer to complete than the *change?*
14. Has the organization set up some way to monitor the progress of the transition?
15. Is the organization prepared to help employees deal with the problems they encounter during the transition or are they pretty much left on their own?

The more negative answers, the more difficult the transition will likely be.

---

[11] Bridges, W., Bridges, S., (2009), *Managing Transitions 3rd Edition, Making the Most of Change,* page 147, Da Campo Press, Philadelphia, PA.

8.8 Develop a Transition Monitoring Team (TMT)

Developing a Transition Monitoring Team is especially important when implementing large changes to a program where the scale of the change may be difficult for the Change Management Action Team (CMAT) to monitor. The TMT is valuable to the process in several ways but the primary benefit is their ability to accurately and effectively provide information from the CMAT to the field and from the field to the CMAT. Communication is the most critical aspect of the entire change process and to have a group of people that are trusted by both sides enables the change process to transition into the program or system much more smoothly.

Building the TMT:

- Make it a relatively small and agile group with no more than 12 members.

- Ensure it encompasses representation from all interested parties of the change.

- Ensure the members want to be there; people who are interested in the project. To do this, explain the task and ask for volunteers.

- Educate the team on their purpose and the scope of their efforts. They are a monitoring team, not a management team. Their purpose is feedback, both to CMAT and the workforce.

- What information, skills or assistance do people need to ensure the team's success?

Define the Charter of the TMT:

- They are to find out the effects the transition is having on people.

- Ensure accurate and timely communication between the CMAT and the workforce and from the workforce to the CMAT is getting through.

- Discover if there are any groups having particular trouble in the transition.

- Determine the approach the TMT will use: 1) Reporting issues that people come to them with, 2) Sending members around to interview people or 3) a combination of both.

- Determine if there are any policies, practices or structures impeding the transition.

Activities of the TMT:

- The TMT should meet as long as there are transition issues to keep track of.

- Phase in new people gradually to replace the original TMT if a transition goes beyond a year.

- Conduct a conference call or meeting about every two weeks.

- Have a non-participating facilitator run the meetings.

- Limit the focus of the TMT discussions to matters that have grown directly out of the changes going on in the organization and the transitions that people are in because of them.

- How often and by what means is the TMT to report back to the CMAT.

Benefits of the TMT:

- People's mistrust starts to die out when they discover their worries and difficulties are being recognized, answered and remedied by the CMAT through the TMT.

- Provide feedback to the groups and individuals on specific issues they originally brought to the TMTs attention.

- TMTs often identify problems at an early stage before they become serious issues.

- TMTs are also an effective way to counter rumors because the members of the team are able to disseminate accurate information. Sometime more accepted as truth by the workforce than if coming directly from management.

9.0   Appendix A: Glossary

Change - *involves developing a means of placing something new into a current system or program to address a given problem.*

Change Management – *Considerations and plans to manage internal and external disruptions to an organization or program.*

Criticality - *Criticality relates to the potential consequences of equipment being improperly operated or an activity being incorrectly executed.*

Gap Analysis – *Identification of existing program components, compared to change program requirements.*

Outputs – *Results of a process, plan or activity that is documented and communicated throughout the program or organization.*

Change Safety Assurance – *A safety process of management functions that systematically provides confidence that the organizations change processes are meeting the safety controls identified in the Change Risk Management process and is on track as per the Change Plan.*

Terms of Reference – *A statement of the operational background and organizational profile in deciding composition of the Change Management Action Team and its activities and interactions within the Change Management Plan.*

Transition - *is the result of incorporating change into the system which then impacts the people within a particular program.*

Transition Management – *A detailed process that addresses change from a personal level for the workforce by building a plan that will orient the change implementation by selecting, designing and scheduling events, actions and projects that move people through the transition phases.*

10.0   Appendix B: References and Resources

1. Bridges, W., Bridges, S., (2009), *Managing Transitions 3rd Edition, Making the Most of Change,* Da Campo Press, Lifelong Books, Philadelphia, PA.

2. FAA AC 120-92a. Safety Management Systems
   www.faa.gov/documentLibrary/media/Advisory_Circular/AC%02120-92A.pdf

3. US Forest Service Aviation SMS Guide, dated 6/21/2011
   http://www.fs.fed.us/fire/av_safety/policy/FS%20SMS%20Guide%20FINAL%20Approved.pdf

4. ICAO Safety Management Manual
   www.icao.int/anb/safetymanagement/DOC_9859_FULL_EN.pdf

5. The MITRE Corporation, (2011), Aviation Safety Management Systems SMS II Course Notebook, McLean, VA.

6. ICAO Fatigue Risk Management System
   www.2.icao.int/en/FatigueManagement?FRMS%20Tools/FRMS%20Implementation%20Guide%20for%20Operators%20July%202011.pdf